BURT FRANKLIN: BIBLIOGRAPHY & REFERENCE 389
American Classics in History and Social Science 164

Bibliography
of
CALIFORNIA
LITERATURE
Pre-Gold Rush Period

Bibliography
of
CALIFORNIA
LITERATURE

Pre-Gold Rush Period

JOSEPH GAER, Editor

BURT FRANKLIN
NEW YORK

Published by LENOX HILL Pub. & Dist. Co. (Burt Franklin)
235 East 44th St., New York, N.Y. 10017
Originally Published: 1935
Reprinted: 1970
Printed in the U.S.A.

S.B.N.: 8337-12594
Library of Congress Card Catalog No.: 78-131407
Burt Franklin: Bibliography and Reference Series 389
American Classics in History and Social Science 164
Reprinted from the original edition in the University of Minnesota Librari

TABLE OF CONTENTS

Prefatory Note

Though the student of California Literature
may find little of high literary value in the
printed remains of the pre-gold rush period, that
literature, devoid of the colors of fiction and
the sounds of poetry, is like the dark brooding
soil of winter upon which the varied wild flowers
blossoming through the gold rush period appeared
with such spectacular suddenness.

For historical reasons, the major portion of
the pre-gold rush literature is in Spanish. And
that phase we have attempted to cover as completely
as possible. The French, Dutch, German and English
bibliographies are not so complete. Though there
were Russians in California before the gold rush,
and some writers among them, they have left no
record of their experiences in this State.

The following bibliography is arranged en-
tirely chronologically.

Joseph Gaer

INTRODUCTION

(a) <u>The origin of the name "California"</u>

The origin of the name "California" remains to this day shrouded in mystery.

About fifty years ago Edward Everett Hale chanced upon the word in a Spanish romance, written in 1510, and quickly concluded that he had discovered the origin of the State's name. Dr. George Davidson supported the theory, and fortified it with the conjecture that the Spaniard had invented the word from two Greek roots: <u>kallos</u>, beauty, or <u>kalli</u>, beautiful, and <u>ornis</u>, a <u>bird</u>.

Greek scholars, however, versed in the medieval usage of classical roots as sources of newly coined words, do not support this theory.

Another attempted explanation of the origin of the name is sought in <u>La Chanson de Roland</u>, a great epic of the eleventh century, in which reference is made to the foes of Charles the Great as ***** those of Polune and of Affrike, and those of Califerne.

Other theorizers have retreated still further into the past in search of the name's origin. They found that one of the Caesars had a wife named <u>Calippurnia</u>, and credited her as the inadvertant mother of California's name.

H. H. Bancroft, the California historian, maintains that in 1846 Vallejo and Alvarado agreed that the name came from the words <u>cali forno</u>, meaning either a high hill or a native land. He further adds that E. D. Guilbert of Copula, Sinaloa, informed him in 1878 that an old Indian of his locality called the peninsula "Tchalifalni-al," meaning, the sandy land beyond the waters.

Another writer, L. Lodain, writing in the <u>Booklover</u> for June, 1902, claims that California is

derived from an Arabic word, Kalifat, a province,
which was changed to an Arabic-Spanish compound,
Kalifon, a great province. Finally California was
evolved.

Other theories credit the latin words Calida
and Fornax, heat and furnace, as the parents of
the word.

And the doors have not yet been closed for
further theories and conjectures.

In literature, however, the name "California"
is found for the first time in Montalvo's book--
a book that must head the list of any chronological
bibliography of the works dealing with this State.

b) ## Character of Pre-Gold Rush Literature

Some time before California was found and ex-
plored, it appeared as the fantastic background of
a chapter in a Spanish romance, Las sergas de
Esplandian, written in 1510 by an "Alderman" of
Median del Campo, Garci Rodriguez de Montalvo, by
name.

In Chapter CLVII of this novel, "which deals
with the wonderful and not premeditated aid with
which Queen Calafia, in behalf of the Turks, arrives
at the gates of Constantinople," we find the
following imaginary description of California:

"Let it be known that to the right of the Indies
there was an island, called California, which was
inhabited by black women, without there being a
single man among them, whose mode of life was almost
like that of Amazons. These women were strong of
body, and brave and fiery of heart, and possessed
great strength; the island itself was the most
rugged of rocks and high cliffs which could be found
anywhere in the world; their implements of war were
of solid gold, and also the trimmings of the wild
beasts on which, after having tamed them, they rode;
for there was no other metal in all the island.* * *
On this island, called California, there were many
griffin, due to the great ruggedness of the land,
and the numerous wild beasts that lived there, which
were found in no other part of the world; and during
the period when they had their young, the women of
California disguised themselves, all covered with very

thick pelts, and carried the young animals to their caves and there raised them."

This is the first description of California in fiction.

A period of nearly three and a half centuries elapsed before it again became the background of a work of fiction.

For California, initially known and partly ex- plored toward the middle of the sixteenth century, has produced practically no fiction or verse to depict the lives, thoughts, and struggles of the people who first disturbed the native Indians of the State.

Before the gold rush days, California was little thought of and little known by the people who had colonized the Atlantic seaboard. For a long time Spanish explorers thought of California as an island and their imaginative cartographers so described it.

The early settlers of the State were too pre- occupied with the problems of survival to have troubled with the preservation of their experiences in poetry and fiction. The Spaniards, the Mexicans, the Indians, the Russians, the missionaries, and the occasional traders and explorers have left behind only historical documents. Letters, handed down fro generation to generation, form another source of knowledge regarding the habits and work of Californi of early times. Some men kept diaries, which are de by day, or week by week, records of how they lived, what they did, the kind of people they were, or fact about those with whom they dealt. Official records too, preserved in archives, are a valuable source of historical material concerning California's past.

But they left no record in poetry and in fiction

All the material about California up to 1833 was printed outside the State. For there were no printi presses in California until some time after the Stat came under Mexican sovereignity.

The first press, a poor one, was brought to Monterey in 1833 by Jose Figueroa when he came to take over the Governorship of the State. The follow

ar, Zamorano, California's first printer, pro-
ced on this press the <u>Reglamento Provisional</u> by
vernor Figueroa--the first printed document in
e State.

One of the books produced on this press, in
36, was an arithmetic primer for children, <u>Tablas</u>
<u>ra los Niños que Empiezan a Contar.</u> A copy of this
ok, in all likelihood the only copy extant, is now
the Huntington Library.

Other books printed in the State were devoted
politics, medicine, military information and
ligion.

It is interesting to note that almost up to the
e of the gold rush California had no newspapers.

The <u>Californian</u>, the State's first published
rnal with type imported from Mexico, was estab-
hed in Monterey, in 1846. The following year it
ed to San Francisco, where is merged with the
ifornia and the <u>Star</u>.

In the Californian appeared the first locally
tten fiction, with the publication of: "Punch
nking and Its Effects." (November 3, 1847, Vol.
No. 25)

On March 15, 1848, this paper carried an incon-
cuous item, apparently about an event of very
tle importance. It related about the finding
gold at Captain Sutter's saw mill.

J.G.

Bibliography

of

CALIFORNIA LITERATURE

PRE-GOLD RUSH PERIOD

S P A N I S H   P H A S E

Spanish Bibliography

Montalvo (Garci Rodríguez de), <u>Las sergas de Esplandián.</u> Sevilla 1510. This book forms the fifth of a series called the Amadís de Gaula (1508), edited by Montalvo. Montalvo edited the first three books of this series; the fourth and fifth he wrote himself. "The name 'California' appears first in this once popular book." California is described as an island inhabited by Amazons (women).

Acosta (Josef de), <u>Historia natural y moral de las Indias.</u> Sevilla, 1590.

Herrera (Antonio de), <u>Descripción de las Indias occidentales.</u> 4 vols. and index, Madrid, En la Oficina Real de Nicolas Rodriguez franco, 1601.

Herrera (Antonio de), <u>Historia general de los hechos de los caste-llanos en las islas i tierra firme del mar océano.</u> Madrid, 1601.

scensión (Antonio de la), <u>Descubrimiento de California.</u> 1620.

íaz del Castillo (Bernal), <u>Historia verdadera de la conquista de la Nueva España.</u> Madrid, 1632.

icolo (Francisco María), <u>Informe del estado de la nueva cristiandad de California.</u> 16 p., Madrid, 1701

mérica, <u>Descripción.</u> 1710.

rquemada, (Juan de), <u>Primera (segunda, tercera) parte de los veinte i un libros rituales i monarquía indiana, con el origen y guerras de los indios occidentales de sus poblaciones (sic), descubrimiento, conquista, conversión y otras cosas maravillo-sas de la mesma tierra.</u> 768, 623, 634 p., Madrid, Nicolás Rodríguez franco, 1723. California, Vol. I, pp. 682-727.

ceta del gobierno de México. 1728-1821.

García (Gregorio), <u>Origen de los indios de el nuevo mundo, e Indias occidentales, averiguado con discurso de opiniones por el Padre Presentado Fr. Gregorio García.</u> 336 p. Madrid Francisco Martínez, 1729. California, pp. 289, 295, 304.

González Cabrera Bueno, (Joseph), <u>Navegación especulativa y práctica con la explicación de algunos instrumentos que están más en uso en los navegantes con las reglas necesarias para su verdadero uso.</u> 392 p. Manila, Convent de Nuestra Señora de los Angeles, 1734. "For many years this was the chief and standard authority used by Spanish navigators."

Consag (Fernando), <u>Carta del Padre Fernando Consag de la Compañia de Jesús, visitador de las misiones de Californias</u> 43 p. San Ignacio, 1748.

Balthassar (Juan Antonio), <u>Carta del Padre Provincial Juan Antonio Balthassar, en que da noticia de la exemplar vida, religiosas, virtudes y apostólicos trabajos del fervoroso misionero el Ven. Padre Francisco María Picolo.</u> 88 p. México, 1752.

Villavicencio (Juan Joseph de), <u>Vida y virtudes de el venerable y apostólico Padre Juan de Ugarte, de la Compañía de Jesús misionero de las islas Californias, y uno de sus primeros conquistadores.</u> 214 p. México, Colegio de San Ildefonso, 1752.

<u>Apostólicos afanes de la Compañía de Jesús.</u> Barcelona, 1754. Ascribed to Padre José Ortega.

Venegas (Miguel), <u>El apóstol Mariano representado en la vida del V. Padre Juan María de Salvatierra, de la Compañía de Jesús, fervoroso misionero en la provincia de Nueva España, y conquistador apostólico de las Californias.</u> 316 p. México, Imprenta de Doña María de Ribera, 1754.

Venegas (Miguel), <u>Noticia de la California y de su conquista temporal y espiritual hasta el tiempo presente.</u> Madrid, 1757, Manuel Fernández. 3 vols., 240, 564, 436 p.

Zevallos (Francisco), Carta del Padre Provincial Francisco Zevallos sobre la apostólica vida y virtudes de Padre Fernando Konsag, insigne misionero de la California. 31 p. México, Colegio de San Ildefonso, 1764.

Amador (Pedro), Expediente de servicios. 1765-91.

Gálvez (José de), Correspondencia con el Padre Lasuen. 1768.

Lasuen (Fermín Francisco), Cartas al visitador general Gálvez. 1768.

Gálvez (José de), Escritos sueltos del visitador general. 1768-70.

Portolá (Gaspar), Diario del viage a la California. 1769.

Fages (Pedro), Voyage en Californie. 1769.

Fages (Pedro), Instrucción para su viage a California. 1769.

Crespí (Juan), Primera espedición de tierra al descubrimiento del puerto de San Diego. 1769.

Crespí (Juan), Viage de la espedición de tierra de San Diego a Monterey. 1769.

Vallejo (Mariano G.), Documentos para la historia de California. 1769-1850.

San Carlos, Manifiesto de su cargamento para California. 1769.

Cañizares (José), Diario de 1769.

Junta primera de guerra en Monterey. 1769.

Gálvez (José de), Instrucción que ha de observar Don Vicente Vila. 1769.

Galvez (José de), <u>Instrucción que ha de observar el teniente Don Pedro Fages.</u> 1769.

Ortega (José Francisco), <u>Correspondencia.</u>

Ortega (José Francisco), <u>Fragmento de 1769.</u>

Constansó (Miguel), <u>Diario histórico de los viages de mar y tierra hechos al norte de la California.</u> México, 1770. 56 p. English translation: London, A. Dalrymple, 1790. "Of the utmost importance, being the first book that relates exclusively to California." Contains a complete account of the Portola expedition. Also an English translation in "Land of Sunshine," Los Angeles, June, July, 1901.

<u>Estracto de noticias del Puerto de Monterey, de las misiones y presidios...,</u> 1770. 8 p. Reprinted in Palou's "Vida de Serra," 1781. English translation in "Land of Sunshine," July, 1901.

Lorenzana (Francisco Antonio), <u>Historia de Nueva España.</u> 400 p. México, 1770. Voyage of Cortés and report of all of the expeditions to California up to 1769. pp. 322-28.

Armona (Matías), <u>Carta de 1770.</u>

<u>Expediente sobre el modo de dividirse las misiones.</u> 1770.

Dumetz (Francisco), <u>Cartas del Padre misionero.</u> 1771-1811.

Bucareli (Virrey), <u>Comunicaciones al comandante general y gobernador de California.</u> 1772-79.

Falou (Francisco), <u>Fondo piadoso de misiones de California.</u> 1772.

Reglamento e instrucción para los presidios. 1772. Madrid, Juan de San Martín. California presidios on pp. 119-122.

Crespí (Juan), Diario del registro de San Francisco. 1772.

Pérez (Juan), Formulario, escripturas de posesión. 1773.

Pérez (Juan), Instrucción que el virrey dió a los comandantes de buques de exploración. 1773.

Palou (Francisco), Circular sobre informes de misiones. 1773.

Palou (Francisco), Informe que por el mes de diciembre de 1773 hizo al Virrey Bucareli.

Palou (Francisco), Informe de 10 diciembre. 1773.

Serra (Junípero), Representación 13 mayo, 1773.

Serra (Junípero), Representación 21 mayo, 1773.

Serra (Junípero), Memorial de 22 de abril, 1773, sobre suministraciones a los establecimientos de California.

Californias, Reglamento provisional. 1773.

Bucareli (Virrey), Providencias del virrey. 1773.

Bucareli (Virrey), Instrucción al comandante de Californias. 1773.

Bucareli (Virrey), Instrucción del Virrey 17 agosto, 1773.

Eche, Respuesta 30 de junio, 1773.

Eche, Parecer 14 de junio, 1773.

Reglamento para el gobierno de la provincia de Californias. 38 p. México, D. Felipe de Zuñiga y Ontiveros, 1784. "The earliest collection of decrees and ordinances prepared for the government of Upper California." (Cowan)

Crespí (Juan), Diario de la expedición de marzo, 1774.

Serra (Junípero), Informe de 1774.

Rivera y Moncada (Fernando), Diligencias en la toma de posesión del mando. 1774.

Maurelle (Francisco Antonio), Compendio de noticias. 1774.

Anza (Juan Bautista), Descubrimiento de Sonora a California. 1774.

Ortega (José Francisco), Comunicaciones del comandante de San Diego a Rivera y Moncada. 1774-76.

Bucareli (Virrey), Instrucción del virrey, 30 setiembre, 1774.

Peña (Tomás), Diario del viage de Pérez. 1774.

Pérez (Juan), Relación del viage. 1774.

Pérez (Juan), Tabla diaria. 1774.

Neve (Felipe), Correspondencia miscelánea del Gobernador. 1775.

Font (Pedro), Journal of a Journey from Sonora to Monterey. 177

Fuster (Vicente), Registro de defunciones. 1775.

Ortega (José Francisco), Informe de 30 noviembre. 1775.

Serra (Junípero), _Informe de 5 de febrero, 1775._

Heceta (Bruno), _Diario del viage de 1775._

Heceta (Bruno), _Segunda exploración._ 1775.

Heceta (Bruno), _Viage de 1775._

Rivera y Moncada (Fernando), _Merced de tierras al soldado Manuel Butrón._ 1775.

Rivera y Moncada (Fernando), _Carta al Padre Serra._ 1775.

Bodega y Caudra (Juan Francisco), _Viage de 1775._

Bodega y Caudra (Juan Francisco), _Comento de la navegación._ 1775.

Maurelle (Francisco Antonio), _Diario del viage de la Sonora._ 1775.

Maurelle (Francisco Antonio), _Journal of a Voyage in 1775._

Anza (Juan Bautista), _Diario de una expedición desde Sonora a San Francisco, California, 1775-76._

Serra (Junípero), _Notas de 1776._

Costansó (Miguel), _Diario histórico de los viages de mar y tierra hechos al norte de California._ 1776.

Serra (Junípero), _Correspondencia._ 1777-82.

Gómez (José), _Diario curioso._ 1777.

Moraga (Gabriel), _Cartas._

Moraga (José Joaquín), Informe de 1777 sobre cosas de San Francisco.

Murguía (José Antonio), and de la Peña (Tomás), Informe de Santa Clara. 1777.

Sal (Hermenegildo), Cartas misceláneas. 1777-1800.

Croix (Teodoro), Comunicaciones del comandante general de provincias internas al gobernador de California, 1777.

Serra (Junípero), Correspondencia. 1777-82.

Estado general de las misiones. 28 p. Madrid, Benito Cano, 1788. Contains a list of the missions in California.

Neve (Felipe), Informe sobre reglamento. 1778.

San Antonio, Documentos sueltos. 1779.

Neve (Felipe), Reglamento e instrucción. 1779.

Maurelle (Francisco Antonio), Navegación. 1779.

Bodega y Caudra (Juan Francisco), Segunda salida. 1779.

Bodega y Caudra (Juan Francisco), Navegación y descubrimiento. 1779.

Arteaga (Ignacio), Tercera exploración. 1779.

Croix (Teodoro), Instrucciones al Capitán Rivera. 1779.

Palou (Francisco), Comunicación al presidente sobre raciones. 1781.

Neve (Felipe), <u>Instrucción para la fundación de Los Angeles.</u>
1781.

Fages (Pedro), <u>Correspondencia del comandante y gobernador.</u>
1781.

Croix (Teodoro), <u>Instrucción sobre donativos en California</u>
<u>para la guerra con Inglaterra.</u> 1781.

<u>Investigación sobre la muerte de los religiosos enviados a la</u>
<u>reducción de los gentiles de Río Colorado.</u> 1781.

González (Diego), <u>Cartas del teniente.</u> 1781.

Los Angeles, <u>Padrón.</u> 1781.

Santa Bárbara, <u>Correspondencia entre Virrey, Guardián y otros,</u>
<u>sobre padres para las nuevas misiones del canal.</u> 1781.

Zúñiga (José), <u>Cartas del comandante de San Diego.</u> 1781-95.

Neve (Felipe), <u>Instrucción que ha de gobernar al comandante</u>
<u>de Santa Bárbara.</u> 1782.

Neve (Felipe), <u>Instrucción al Ayudante Inspector Soler.</u> 1782.

Neve (Felipe), <u>Instrucción a Fages sobre gobierno interino.</u> 1782.

Croix (Teodoro), <u>Disposiciones para la guerra a los Yumas.</u> 1782.

<u>Arancel de precios.</u> 1782.

Carrillo (Mariano), <u>Testamento e inventario.</u> 1782.

Moraga (José Joaquín), <u>Instrucción y orden que debe observar</u>
<u>el cabo de escolta de San José.</u> 1782.

Fagas (Pedro), Instrucciones al comandante interino de Monterey. 1783.

Palou (Francisco), Letter of August 15, 1783.

Estrada (José Mariano), Correspondencia desde 1783.

Lasuen (Fermín Francisco), Informe de 1783.

Velásquez (José), Diario y mapa de un reconocimiento. 1783.

Gálvez (Virrey), Comunicaciones al gobernador de California. 1783-85.

Lasuen (Fermín Francisco), Carta de 1784.

Lasso de la Vega (José Ramón), Escritos del alférez. 1784.

Palou (Francisco), Defunción del Padre Junípero Serra. 1784.

Nayarit, Informe de la audiencia de Guadalajara. 1784.

Fages (Pedro), Representación contra los frailes. 1785.

Goycoechea (Felipe), Escritos del comandante de Santa Bárbara 1785-1806.

Gómez (Juan), Documentos para la historia de California. 1785-1850.

Sánchez, Fidalgo, and Costansó, Informe sobre auxilios que se propone enviar a California. 1785.

Sancho (Juan), Informe del guardián al virrey. 1785.

Velásquez (José), Relación del viage que hizo el Gobernador Fages. 1785.

Palou (Francisco), Informe sobre quejas del gobernador. 1785.

Gálvez (Virrey), Instrucción formada en virtud de real orden de S.M., que se dirige al Senor Comandante...Jacob Ugarte. 56 p. México, 1786.

Gálvez (Virrey), Instrucciones al Gobernador Fages. 1786.

Los Angeles, Repartición de solares y suertes. 1786.

Alcedo (Antonio de), Diccionario geográfico histórico de las Indias occidentales. 1786-89.

Peña (Tomás), Cargo de homicidio contra el padre. 1786-95.

Ortega (José Francisco), Memorial sobre sus méritos y servicios militares. 1786.

Santa Bárbara, Memorias de efectos remitidos a la misión. 1786-1810.

Palou (Francisco), Relación histórica de la vida de Junípero Serra. México, 1787.

Soler (Nicolás), Parecer sobre comercio con el buque de China. 1787.

Soler (Nicolás), Informe sobre policía y gobierno. 1787.

Fages (Pedro), Informe general de misiones. 1787.

Fages (Pedro), Informe sobre comercio con buques de China. 1787.

Fages (Pedro), Instrucción para el cabo de escolta de Angeles. 1787.

Fages (Pedro), Instruccion para la escolta de S. Miguel. 1787.

Fages (Pedro), Instrucción para la escolta de Purísima. 1788.

Arancel de precios. 1788.

Martínez (Estevan José), and Gonzalo López de Haro, Cuarta exploración. 1788.

Informe de lo más peculiar de la Nueva California. 1789.

Revilla Gigedo (Virrey), Instrucción que dejó escrita. 1789-94.

Revilla Gigedo (Virrey), Comunicaciones al gobernador de California. 1790-94.

Costansó (Miguel), Historical Journal of the Expeditions by Sea and Land to the North of California. 1790.

Fidalgo (Salvador), Tabla de descubrimientos de 1790.

Fidalgo (Salvador), Viage de 1790.

Nava (Pedro), Comunicaciones del comandante general de provincias internas. 1791.

Romeau (José Antonio), Cartas al Padre Presidente Lasuen. 1791.

Recopilación de leyes de los reynos de las Indias mandadas imprimir y publicar por Carlos II. 1791.

Lasuen (Fermín Francisco), Carta sobre fundación de misiones. 1791.

Junta de 5 de abril de 1791 en Monterey.

López (Baldomero), and Salazar (Isidro Alonso), <u>Carta de los padres de Santa Cruz.</u> 1791.

Arrillaga (José Joaquín), <u>Hojas de servicio.</u> 1791-98.

Fages (Pedro), <u>Informes particulares al Gobernador Romeu.</u> 1791.

Fages (Pedro), <u>Papel de varios puntos.</u> 1791.

Sal (Hermenegildo), <u>Reconocimiento de la misión de Santa Cruz.</u> 1791.

Sal (Hermenegildo), <u>Instrucción al cabo de la escolta de Santa Cruz.</u> 1791.

Espinosa (José de), <u>Relación del viage hecho por las goletas Sutil y Mexicana en el año de 1792.</u> 185 p. Madrid, Imprenta real, 1802. English translation: Argonaut Press, 1930.

Arricivita (J.D.), <u>Crónica seráfica y apostólica.</u> México, 1792. 606 p. Part II contains references to Alta California.

Sal (Hermenegildo), <u>Informes sobre los edificios de San Francisco.</u> 1792.

Lasuen (Fermín Francisco), <u>Informes bienales de las misiones.</u> 1793-1802.

Revilla Gigedo (Virrey), <u>Carta de 27 diciembre, 1793.</u>

Revilla Gigedo (Virrey), <u>Carta sobre misiones.</u> 1793.

Revilla Gigedo (Virrey), <u>Informe de 12 abril.</u> 1793.

Arrillaga (José Joaquín), Informe al virrey aobre defensas. 1793.

Arrillaga (José Joaquín), Borrador de carta a Vancouver. 1793.

Grijalva (Juan Pablo), Cartas del teniente. 1794-1806.

Grajera (Antonio), Escritos del comandante de San Diego. 1794-99.

Costansó (Miguel), Informe sobre el proyecto de fortificar los presidios de California. 1794.

Mugártegui (Pablo), Carta al Padre Lasuen. 1794.

Sales (Luis), Noticias de Californias. Valencia, 1794. 3 vols. 104, 96, 104 p.

Branciforte (Virrey), Instrucción. 1794-97.

Branciforte (Virrey), Varios oficios. 1794-98.

Arrillaga (José Joaquín), Papel de puntos para conocimiento del gobernador. 1794.

Catalá (Magin), Carta sobre Nootka. 1794.

Amador (Pedro), Reconocimiento desde Santa Cruz hasta San Francisco. 1795.

Ortega (Felipe María), Diario que forma. 1795.

Branciforte (Virrey), A Borica sobre baterías de San Francisco 1795.

Branciforte (Virrey), Informe del real tribunal sobre la fundación. 1795.

Carrillo (Raimundo), *Papeles del capitán.* 1795.

Sánchez, Fidalgo, and Costansó, *Informe sobre auxilios que se propone enviar a California.* 1795.

al (Hermenegildo), *Informe de los parages que se han reconocido en la alameda.* 1795.

érez Fernández (José), *Cuenta general de la habilitación de Monterey.* 1796.

eñan (José F. de P.), *Respuesta al virrey sobre condición de cosas en California.* 1796.

alazar (Alonso Isidro), *Condición actual de California.* 1796.

al (Hermenegildo), *Informe.* 1796.

suen (Fermín Francisco), *Informe sobre sitios para nuevas misiones.* 1796.

rica (Diego), *Informe de nuevas misiones.* 1796.

rica (Diego), *Informe sobre comunicación con Nuevo México.* 1796.

rica (Diego), *Proyecto sobre división de Californias.* 1796.

rdoba (Alberto), *Informe al virrey sobre defensas de California.* 1796.

rdoba (Alberto), *Informe acerca del sitio de Branciforte.* 1796.

doba (Alberto), *Cartas del ingeniero.* 1796-98.

Alberni (Pedro), <u>Comunicaciones del teniente coronel.</u> 1796-1800

Alberni (Pedro), <u>Parecer sobre el sitio de Branciforte.</u> 1796.

Amador (Pedro), <u>Expedición contra los gentiles Sacalanes.</u> 1796.

Font (José), <u>Varios escritos del teniente.</u> 1796.

Calleja (Virrey), <u>Respuesta del guardián al virrey sobre proyectos de California.</u> 1797.

<u>Guía de forasteros.</u> 1797.

Mugártegui (Pablo), and de la Peña (Tomás), <u>Parecer sobre el establecimiento de un convento en San Francisco.</u> 1797.

Lasuen (Fermín Francisco), <u>Fundación de misiones.</u> 1797.

Amador (Pedro), <u>Prevenciones al cabo de la escolta de San José.</u> 1797.

Amador (Pedro), <u>Diario de la expedición para fundar la misión de San José.</u> 1797.

Arguello (José), <u>Relación de lo que declararon los gentiles Sacalanes.</u> 1797.

Arguello (José), <u>Relación que formó sobre indios huídos de San Francisco.</u> 1797.

Arguello (José), <u>Cartas de un gobernador de las Californias.</u>

Borica (Diego), <u>Instrucción de dirigir la fundación de Branciforte.</u> 1797.

Borica (Diego), <u>Instrucción para la excolta de San Juan Bautista.</u> 1797.

Borica (Diego), Castigos que han de sufrir los indios. 1797.

Pío VI, Breve apostólico en que se les concede varias gracias a los misioneros. 1797.

Cáraba (Manuel), Informe del habilitado general. 1797.

Branciforte (villa de), El discretorio de San Fernando al virrey. 1797.

Branciforte (villa de), Dictamen del fiscal sobre fundación. 1797.

San José, Cuestión de límites. 1797-1801.

al (Hermenegildo), Respuesta a las quince preguntas. 1798.

odríguez (Manuel), Respuesta a las quince preguntas. 1798.

apis (Estevan), Expedición a Calahuasa. 1798.

oycoechea (Felipe), Diario de exploración. 1798.

oycoechea (Felipe), Respuesta a las quince preguntas sobre abusos de misioneros. 1798.

guello (José), Informe sobre Rancho del Rey en San Francisco. 1798.

guello (José), Respuesta a las quince preguntas sobre abusos de misioneros. 1798.

rnández (Manuel), Carta del padre ministro de Santa Cruz. 1798.

Horra (Antonio de la Concepción), Representación al virrey contra los misioneros de California. 1798.

de la Poña (Tomás), Petición del guardián sobre límites de Santa Clara. 1798.

El viagero universal. Madrid, Villalpando, 1799. Vol. 26, 384 p. Description of Alta California with maps, pp. 5-189.

Castro (Macario), Diario de su expedición a las rancherías. 1799.

Lull (Miguel), Exposición del Padre Guardián sobre reducción de misioneros en California. 1799.

Grajera (Antonio), Respuesta a las quince preguntas. 1799.

Lasuen (Fermín Francisco), Representación sobre los puntos representados al gobierno por el Padre Antonio de la Concepción. 1800.

Malaspina (Alejandro) and de Bustamante (José), Carta al Padre Lasuen, y respuesta.

Marquina (Virrey), Comunicaciones al gobernador de California. 1800.

Tapis (Estevan), and Juan Cortés, Réplica de los ministros de Santa Bárbara. 1800.

Amador (Pedro), Salida contra indios gentiles. 1800.

Azanza (Virrey), Instrucción. 1800.

Carrillo (Raimundo), Instrucción que observará el comandante de escolta de Santa Inés.

Carrillo (Raimundo), <u>Los edificios de Monterey.</u> 1800.

Rosas (José Antonio), <u>Causa criminal.</u> 1800-01.

Nava (Pedro), <u>Informe sobre proyecto de abrir caminos entre California y Nuevo Mexico.</u> 1801.

Borbon, <u>Parecer del fiscal sobre el proyecto de abrir comunicación entre California y Nuevo México.</u> 1801.

Gasol (José), <u>Expediente sobre capellanes de presidios.</u> 1802.

Goycoechea (Felipe), <u>Oficio instructivo para el Teniente R. Carrillo.</u> 1802.

Tapis (Estevan), <u>Informes bienales de misiones.</u> 1803-10.

Rodríguez (Manuel), <u>Lo acaecido con tripulantes de la Byrd.</u> 1803.

Arrillaga (José Joaquín), <u>Informe sobre el estado de indios.</u> 1804.

Peralta (Luis), <u>Diario de una expedición contra gentiles.</u> 1805.

Goycoechea (Felipe), <u>Medios para el fomento de Californias.</u> 1805.

Sola (Pablo Vicente), <u>Correspondencia del gobernador.</u> 1805-22.

Vallejo (Mariano G.), and Juan R. Cooper, <u>Varios libros de cuentas.</u> 1805-51.

<u>Expediente sobre las enfermedades de la tierra.</u> 1805.

Gasol (José), <u>Letras patentes del Padre Guardián.</u> 1806.

Arrillaga (José Joaquín), Preceptos generales para comandante
1806.

Arrillaga (José Joaquín), Relación del estado que guardan los
presidios y pueblos. 1806.

San José, Libro de patentes. 1806-24.

Muñoz (Pedro), Diario de la expedición hecha por Don Gabriel
Moraga al Tular. 1806.

Zalvidea (José María), Diario de una expedición. 1806.

Arguello (José), Instrucción que ha de observar el Teniente
Luis Arguello en San Francisco. 1806.

Abella (Ramón), Noticia de una batalla entre cristianos y
gentiles. 1807.

Tapis (Estevan), Noticias presentadas al Gobernador Arrillaga
1808.

Payeras (Mariano), Comunicación sobre la misión de la Purísima
1810.

Viader (José), Diario o noticia del viage. 1810.

Viader (José), Diario de una entrada al Río de San Joaquín.
1810.

Moraga (Gabriel), Diario de su expedición al Puerto de
Bodega. 1810.

San Buenaventura, suministraciones al presidio. 1810-20.

Tapis (Estevan), Parecer sobre repartimientos de indios. 1810

Cancelada (Juan López), Verdad sabida. 1811.

Garijo (Agustín), Carta del Padre Guardián en que da noticia de la revolución. 1811.

Cancelada (Juan López), Ruina de la Nueva España. 1811.

Abella (Ramón), Diario de un registro de los ríos grandes. 1811.

Señan, (José F. de P.), Respuesta al virrey sobre condición de cosas en California.

Señan, (José F. de P.), Informes bienales de misiones. 1811-14.

Fondo Piadoso de Californias, Demostración de los sinodos que adeuda a los religiosos. 1811-34.

Establecimientos rusos en California. 1812.

Indios, Interrogatorio del supreme gobierno sobre costumbres. 1812.

Ayuntamientos, Decreto de las cortes. 1812.

Cancelada (Juan López), El télegrafo mexicano. 1813.

Decreto de cortes. 1813.

Calleja (Virrey), Comunicaciones al gobernador de California. 1813-16.

Purísima, Petición de los padres sobre traslado de la misión. 1813.

arría (Vicente Francisco), Exhortación pastoral. 1813.

Cabot (Juan), Expedición al valle de los tulares. 1814.

Arrillaga (José Joaquín), Testamento. 1814.

Carrillo (Carlos Antonio), Pedimento de reos. 1814.

Señan (José F. de P.), Circular del Vicario Foráneo. 1815.

Torre (Estevan de la), Reminiscencias. 1815-48.

Indios, Contestación al interrogatorio de 1812 por el
    presidente y los padres sobre costumbres. 1815.

Eliot de Castro (Juan), Papeles tocantes a su arrestación. 1815.

San Salvador (Agustín Pomposo Fernández de), Los jesuitas
    quitados y restituidos al mundo. Historia de la antigua
    California. Mexico, Mariano Ontiveros, 1816. 165 p.

Martínez (Ignacio), Entrada a las rancherías del Tular. 1816.

Los Angeles, Lista de los pobladores, inválidos, y vecinos.
    1816.

Arguello (Gervasio), Observaciones. 1816.

Eestard (Buenaventura), Pastoral del comisario general de
    Indias. 1816.

Sola (Pablo Vicente), Defensa del Padre Quintana y otros. 1816.

Sola (Pablo Vicente), Instrucciones al comisionado de
    Branciforte. 1816.

Sola (Pablo Vicente), Informe general al virrey sobre
    defensas. 1817.

Payeras (Mariano), Instrucción del Vicario Foráneo. 1817.

Protesta de los padres contra gabelas. 1817.

Sarría (Vicente Francisco), Carta pastoral. 1817.

Payeras (Mariano), Circular del presidente. 1817.

Sarría (Vicente Francisco), Informe del comisario prefecto sobre los frailes de California. 1817.

Alviso (José Antonio), Documentos para la historia de California. 1817-50.

Avila (Antonio), y otros, Papeles tocantes a su sedición.

Payeras (Mariano), Circular a los padres. 1818.

Sola (Pablo Vicente), Informe al General Cruz sobre los insurgentes. 1818.

Sola (Pablo Vicente), Informe suplementario sobre los insurgentes. 1818.

Sola (Pablo Vicente), Instrucción general a los comandantes, contra los insurgentes. 1818.

Sola (Pablo Vicente), Observaciones en la visita desde San Francisco hasta San Diego. 1818.

Sola (Pablo Vicente), Noticia de lo acaecido en este puerto de Monterey, rebeldes de Buenos Aires. 1818.

Los Angeles, Instancia de regidores y vecinos sobre tierras. 1819.

Payeras (Mariano), Petición al gobernador. 1819.

Sarría (Vicente Francisco), _Informe de misiones._ 1819.

Venadito (Virrey), _Comunicaciones al gobernador de California._ 1819.

Guerra y Noriega (José), _Determinación sobre su ida a México, e instrucción._ 1819.

Olvera (Agustín), _Varias cartas._

López (Baldomero), and Salazar (Isidro Alonso), _Carta de los padres de Santa Cruz._

López (Baldomero), _Quejas del Padre Guardián al virrey._ 1819.

Payeras (Mariano), _Circular a los padres._ 1819.

López (Baldomero), _El guardián al presidente sobre cesión de misiones._ 1820.

Sánchez (José Antonio), _Correspondencia del alférez._

Constitución española de 1812, bandos del virrey sobre su jura. 1820.

López (Baldomero), _El guardián a los padres, prohibiendo el uso de carruajes._ 1820.

Estudillo (José María), _Informe sobre oficios de capellán._ 1820.

Estudillo (José María), _Informe sobre los frailes._ 1820.

Payeras (Mariano), _Informe por el comisario prefecto del actual estado de los 19 misiones._ 1820.

Payeras (Mariano), _Informes bienales de misiones._ 1820.

Payeras (Mariano), Memorial a los padres, sobre la cesión de las nueve misiones del sur. 1820.

Payeras (Mariano), Memorial de 2 de junio. 1820.

Itúrbide (Agustín), Cartas de los señores generales. 1821.

Guadalajara, Gaceta de gobierno. 1821.

Marquínez (Marcelino), Cartas del padre al Gobernador Sola. 1821.

Gaceta imperial de México. 1821-23.

Payeras (Mariano), Memorial sobre nueva iglesia en Los Angeles. 1821.

Payeras (Mariano), Memorial a los padres. 1821.

Payeras (Mariano), Representación sobre innovaciones del señor gobernador. 1821.

Payeras (Mariano), Circular en que prohibe el uso de carruajes. 1821.

Payeras (Mariano), Cordillera sobre suministración de víveres. 1821.

Payeras (Mariano), Dos circulares sobre contrata con McCulloch, Hartnell y Cía. 1822.

Medina (Antonio), Memoria presentada al soberano congreso mexicano por el secretario de estado y del despacho de marina. México, Valdés, 1822. 29 p.

Pérez (Eulalia), Una vieja y sus recuerdos.

Fernandez de San Vicente (Agustín), Comunicaciones del canónigo. 1822.

Sánchez (José Antonio), Diario de la caminata que hizo el Padre Prefecto Payeras, San Diego a San Gabriel. 1822.

Ayala (Tadeo Ortiz), Resumen de la estadística del imp. mex. 1822.

Sola (Pablo Vicente), Prevenciones sobre elección de diputado. 1822.

Espinosa (Carlos), Exposición que hizo sobre las provincias de Sonora, Sinaloa, y ambas Californias. México, M. Ontiveros, 1823. 44 p.

Sánchez (José Antonio), Diario de la expedición, nueva planta de San Francisco. 1823.

Altimira (José), Diario de la expedición. 1823.

Bustamante (Carlos María), Cuadro histórico de la revolución mexicana. 1823-27.

Altimira (José), Journal of a Mission-founding Expedition. 1823.

Romero (José), Documentos relativos a su expedición para abrir camino entre Sonora y California. 1823-26.

Ripoll (Antonio), Levantamiento de indios en Santa Bárbara. 1824.

Plan de gobierno provincial. 1824.

Decreto del congreso mejicano sobre colonización. 1824.

Reglamento de contribuciones sobre licores. 1824.

Instrucciones para tribunales de primera instancia. 1824.

Mier y Teran (Manuel de), Memoria del secretario de estado
    y del despacho de la guerra. México, 1825. 21 p.
    Account of affairs in California in 1824.

Compañía asiático-mexicana, plan y reglamento. 1825.

Pacheco (Romualdo), Cartas. 1825-31.

Plan de colonización estrangera. 1825.

Plan de colonización de nacionales. 1825.

Plan para arreglo de misiones. 1825.

Plan político mercantil. 1825.

Dictamen sobre instrucciones al gobernador de Californias.
    1825.

Echeandía (José María), Escritos sueltos del comandante
    general. 1825-33.

Fitch (Henry D. and Josefa C.), Documentos para la historia
    de California.

Echeandía (José Mariá), Decreto de emancipación a favor de
    los neófitos. 1826.

Sánchez (José Antonio), Journal of the Enterprise Against
    the Cosemenes. 1826.

Castro (José), Correspondencia oficial y particular del
    General. 1826-46.

Correo de la federación. 1826.

Amigo del pueblo. 1827.

Iniciativo de ley. 1827.

Herrera (José Mariá), Causa contra el comisario de California.
    1827.

Los Angeles, Reglamento de policía. 1827.

Junta de fomento de Californias, colección de los trabajos.
    1827.

Reglamento sobre ganados. 1827.

Pico (Andrés), Papeles de misiones. 1828-46.

Rubio (Francisco), Causa criminal por asesinato y estupro.
    1828-31.

Echeandía (José Mariá), Bando sobre elecciones. 1828.

Españoles, Lista de los que han prestado juramento. 1828.

Arguello (Luis Antonio), Hoja de servicios hasta 1828.

Bandini (Juan), Carta histórica y descriptiva de California.
    1828.

Atleta (el) México. 1829.

Piña (Joaquín), Diario de la espedición al valle de San José.
    1829.

Estrada (José Ramón), Lista de extrangeros en Monterey.
    1829.

Echeandía (José María), Plan para convertir en pueblos las misiones. 1829.

Sánchez (José Antonio), Campana contra Estanislao. 1829.

San José, Petición del ayuntamiento en favor de los frailes españoles. 1829.

Solis (Joaquín), Manifiesto al público, o sea plan de revolución. 1829.

Solis (Joaquín), Proceso instruído contra --- y otros revolucionarios. 1829.

Martínez (Ignacio), Defensa dirigida al comandante general. 1830.

Sarría (Vicente Francisco), Defensa del Padre Luis Martínez. 1830.

Fitch (Henry D.), Causa criminal por matrimonio nulo. 1830.

Bustamante (Anastasio), Escritos del senor presidente tocante a California. 1830-32.

Guerra y Noriega (José), Ocurrencias curiosas de 1830-31.

Alaman (Lucas), Sucesos de California en 1831.

Pronunciamiento de San Diego contra Victoria. 1831.

Atanasio, Causa criminal contra el indio. 1831.

Carrillo (Carlos Antonio), Exposición...sobre arreglo y administración del fondo piadoso. Mexico, C. Alejandro Valdés, 1831.

Bandini (Juan), Contestación a la alocución de Victoria. 1831.

Bermúdez (J.M.), Verdadera causa de la revolución. 1831.

Pico (Pió), Protesta al manifiesto de Don Manuel Victoria. 1831.

Carrillo (Carlos Antonio), Cartas del diputado de Alta California. 1831-32.

Figueroa (José), Informe al ministro de guerra sobre acontecimientos de 1831-32.

Figueroa (José), Instrucciones generales para el gobierno de California.

Durán (Narciso), Notas y comentarios al bando de Echeandía sobre misiones. 1831.

Echeandía (José María), Decreto de secularización. 1831.

Gómez (José Joaquín), Cartas. 1831.

Iriarte (Francisco), Contestación a la expresión de agravios. 1832.

Gutiérrez (Nicolás), Varias cartas del capitán y gefe político. 1832-36.

Echeandía (José María), Reglamento de secularización. 1832.

Figueroa (José), Correspondencia del gefe político. 1832-35

Vallejo (Mariano G.), and Cooper (Juan R.), Varios libros de cuentas.

Vallejo (Mariano G.), and Arguello (Santiago), Expediente sobre las arbitrariedades de Victoria. 1832.

Bandini (Juan), <u>Manifiesto a la diputación sobre ramos de hacienda territorial.</u> 1832.

Alaman (Lucas), <u>Censo de California.</u> 1832.

Sánchez (José Antonio), <u>Notas al reglamento de secularización.</u> 1832.

<u>Pronunciamiento de Monterey contra el plan de San Diego.</u> 1832.

Avila (Juan), <u>Notas Californianas.</u>

Avila (Antonio), y otros, <u>Papeles tocantes a su sedición.</u> 1832.

Bandini (Juan), <u>Apuntes políticos.</u> 1832.

Zamorano (Agustín V.), <u>Proclama que contiene los artículos de las condiciones entre él y Echeandía.</u> 1832.

<u>Compañía extrangera de Monterey, cuaderno de órdenes.</u> 1832.

Guzmán (José María), <u>Breve noticia que da al supremo gobierno del actual estado del territorio de la Alta California.</u> Mexico, Imprenta de la águila, 1833. 8 p.

Bandini (Juan), <u>El diputado de la Alta California a sus comitentes.</u> 1833.

Guerrero (Vicente), <u>Soberano estado de Oajaca.</u> 1833.

Figueroa (José), <u>Prevenciones provisionales para la emancipación de indios.</u> 1833.

<u>Fondo piadoso de Californias, ley y reglamento.</u> México, 1833. 20 p.

Figueroa (José), <u>Anuncia a los californios su llegada.</u>
  Monterey, 1833. The first specimen of California
  printing.

Echeandía (José María), <u>Reglamento para los encargados de
  justicia en las misiones.</u> 1833.

<u>Decreto del congreso mejicano, secularizando las misiones.</u>
  1833.

Durán (Narciso), <u>Crítica sobre las prevenciones de
  emancipación.</u> 1833.

Durán (Narciso), <u>Notas a una circular o bando de Echeandía.</u>
  1833.

Durán (Narciso), <u>Proyectos de secularización.</u> 1833.

Echeandía (José María), <u>Carta que dirige a Don José Figueroa
  en defensa de lo que ha hecho para secularizar las
  misiones.</u> 1833.

Vallejo (Mariano G.), <u>Informe reservado sobre Ross.</u> 1833.

García Diego (Francisco), <u>Carta pastoral contra la costumbre
  de azotar a los indios.</u> 1833.

García Diego (Francisco), <u>Parecer del Padre Fiscal sobre el
  proyecto de secularización.</u> 1833.

Coronel (Ignacio), <u>Cartas de un maestro de escuela.</u> 1834.

Bandini (Juan), <u>Acusaciones contra Angel Ramírez.</u> 1834-37.

Abrego (José), <u>Cartas sobre la colonia de 1834.</u>

Zamorano (Agustín V.), y Cía., <u>Aviso al público.</u> Monterey,1834.
　　Broadside. Announcement by printer of opening of
　　printing office.

<u>Plan de propios y arbitrios para fondos municipales.</u> 1834.

<u>Reglamento provisional para la secularización de las misiones</u>
　　<u>de la Alta California.</u> Monterey, 1834. Broadside.

<u>Reglamento provisional para el gobierno interior de la Ecma.</u>
　　<u>diputación territorial de la Alta California.</u>
　　Monterey, Zamorano, 1834. 16 p. The first book
　　printed in California.

Bonilla (Mariano), <u>Varias cartas.</u> 1834-37.

Figueroa (José), <u>Bando en que publica la resolución de la</u>
　　<u>diputación contra Híjar.</u> 1834.

Figueroa (José), <u>Bando contra Híjar.</u> 1834.

Figueroa (José), <u>Cosas financieras de California.</u> 1834.

Figueroa (José), <u>Discurso de apertura de la diputación.</u> 1834.

Figueroa (José), and others, <u>Convite al baile.</u> Monterey,
　　1834. Broadside.

Híjar (Carlos N.), <u>California in 1834.</u>

Híjar (José María), <u>Instrucciones del gefe político y</u>
　　<u>director de colonización.</u> 1834.

Figueroa (José), <u>Plan de propios y arbitrios.</u> Monterey, 1834.

Bandini (Juan), <u>Información del visitador de aduana.</u> 1835.

Apalátegui y Torres, Averiguación en Sonora del tumulto de Los Angeles. 1835.

Apalátegui y Torres, Causa seguida contra los conspiradores. 1835.

Correo atlántico (El). México, 1835.

Rivera, Nueva colección de leyes. 1835.

Pronunciamiento de Apalátegui en Los Angeles. 1835.

García Diego (Francisco), Reglas que propone padre prefecto para gobierno interior de las ex-misiones. 1835.

San Antonio, Extracto del libro de difuntos. 1835.

Padrés (José María), Protesta que dirige al gefe político. 1835.

Figueroa (José), El comandante general y gefe político de la Alta California a los habitantes del territorio. Monterey, 1835. Broadside.

Figueroa (José), El comandante general y gefe político de Alta California a sus habitantes. 1835.

Figueroa (José), Instrucciones generales para el gobierno de California.

Figueroa (José), Manifiesto a la República Mejicana. Monterey, 1835, C.A.V. Zamorano. 184 p. Second bo printed in California.

Bustamante (Carlos María de), Los tres siglos de México durante el gobierno español. México, Luis Abadíar y Valdés, 1836-38. 4 vols. 281, 185,419, and 281 p

<u>Tablas para los niños que empiezan a contar.</u> Monterey, A. Zamorano, 1836.

Ximeno (D. Rafael), <u>Tabla para los niños que empiezan a contar.</u> Monterey, Zamorano, 1336. Broadside.

Gutiérrez (Nicolás), <u>Comandancia general de la Alta California.</u> Monterey, 1836. Broadside.

Chico (Mariano), <u>El ciudadano, Coronel Mariano Chico, comandante general, inspector y gefe superior político de la Alta California a sus habitantes.</u> Monterey, 1836. Broadside.

Castro (José), <u>La ecselentísima diputación de la Alta California a sus habitantes.</u> Monterey, Nov. 6, 1836. Broadside.

Castro (José), Alvarado (Juan), Buelna (Antonio), and Noriega (José Antonio), <u>En el puerto de Monterey de la Alta California.</u> Monterey, 1836. Broadside. In this proclamation California is declared to be free and independent.

Alvarado (Juan), <u>Coronel de la milicia cívica, gefe superior.., a los habitantes.</u> Monterey, Dec. 20, 1836. Broadside.

sio (Antonio María), <u>Carta sobre combinaciones políticas.</u> 1836.

sio (Antonio María), <u>Carta a Vallejo.</u> 1836.

nico (Mariano), <u>El gefe superior político a los habitantes.</u> Monterey, 1836. Broadside.

nico (Mariano), <u>Discurso pronunciado 20 de mayo.</u> Monterey, 1836. Broadside.

nico (Mariano), <u>Discurso pronunciado 27 de mayo.</u> Monterey, 1836. 2 leaves.

Chico (Mariano), <u>Escritos del gobernador.</u> 1836

Chico (Mariano), <u>Alocución del gobernador a la junta.</u> 1836.

Chico (Mariano), <u>El comandante general y gefe político de Alta California a sus habitabtes.</u> Monterey, 1836. Broadside.

<u>Plan de independencia adoptada por la diputación.</u> 1836.

<u>Plan de independencia californiana.</u> 1836.

Bandini (Juan), <u>Carta a Vallejo sobre revoluciones.</u> 1836.

<u>Junta de guerra y rendición de Monterey.</u> 1836.

Romero (José Mariano), <u>Memorias de un anciano.</u>

Romero (José Mariano), <u>Catecismo de ortología dedicado a los alumnos de la escuela normal de Monterey.</u> Monterey, C.A.V. Zamorano, 1836.

Vallejo (Mariano G.), <u>Proclama en el acto de prestar el juramento.</u> 1836. Monterey; Broadside.

<u>Diputación de la Alta California a sus habitantes.</u> 1836.

Durán (Narciso), <u>Carta al Gobernador Chico.</u> 1836.

Gómez (Juan), <u>Diario de cosas notables.</u> 1836.

Gutiérrez (Nicolás), <u>Carta oficial del gefe político.</u> 1836.

Gutiérrez (Nicolás), <u>Publica el decreto reuniendo los mandos y toma posesion del gobierno político.</u> 1836.

Castillo Negrete (Luis), <u>Consejos al comandante de Santa Bárbara.</u> 1836.

Castillo Negrete (Luis), <u>Exposición que dirige el juez de distrito al ayuntamiento de Los Angeles sobre el plan revolucionario de Monterey.</u> 1836.

Castro (José), <u>Decretos de la diputación erigida en congreso constituyente.</u> Monterey, 1836. A series of 10 decretos printed in the form of broadsides.

Castro, (José), <u>Despacho de coronel expedido a Don Juan B. Alvarado.</u> Monterey, Dec. 11, 1836. Broadside.

Castro (José), <u>Proclama de 13 de noviembre, 1836.</u> Broadside.

Carrillo (Carlos Antonio), <u>Cartas al General Vallejo.</u> 1836.

Carrillo (Carlos Antonio), <u>Correspondencia miscelánea.</u>

Bandini (Juan), <u>Carta a Vallejo sobre revoluciones.</u> 1836.

Alvarado (Juan Bautista), <u>Carta confidencial.</u> 1836.

Alvarado (Juan Bautista), <u>Despacho de capitán a favor de J. J. Vallejo.</u> Monterey, Dec. 12, 1836. Broadside.

Castañares (José María), <u>Causa seguida contra Ana González.</u> 1836.

Vega (José María Luis), <u>Obras sueltas.</u> 1837

Escudero (José Agustín), <u>Noticias estadísticas de Chihuahua.</u> 1837.

Bandini (Juan), <u>Sucesos del sur.</u> 1837.

Bandini (Juan), Discurso ante el ayuntamiento de Los Angeles.
1837.

Alvarado (Juan Bautista), Proclama del gobernador interino.
Monterey, May 10, 1837. Broadside.

Alvarado (Juan Bautista), Comunicaciones al ayuntamiento de
Los Angeles. 1837.

Alvarado (Juan Bautista), Carta en que relata la campaña de
San Fernando. 1837.

Alvarado (Juan Bautista), Manifiesto del gobernador. 1837.

Alvarado (Juan Bautista), El gobernador interino del estado
libri de Alta California a sus habitantes. 1837.

Alvarado (Juan Bautista), Carta en que relata los sucesos
de Los Angeles. 1837.

Carrillo (Carlos Antonio), Discurso al tomar el mando
político en Los Angeles. 1837.

Plan de gobierno adoptado por la diputación en Santa Bárbar
1837.

Instrucciones a que debe sujetarse la comisión nombrada por
este ayuntamiento de Los Angeles. 1837.

Salidas de buques del puerto de San Francisco. 1837.

Vallejo (Mariano G.), Exposición que hace el comandante
general interino de la Alta California al gobernado
de la misma. Sonoma, 1837. 21 p.

Vallejo (Mariano G.), Carta impresa al gobernador. 1837.

Vallejo (Mariano G.), Ordenes de la comandancia general d
la Alta California. Sonoma, 1837-39,

Vallejo (Mariano G.), <u>Proclama.</u> 1837.

Vallejo (Mariano G.), <u>Tres cartas reservadas.</u> 1837.

Solano (Francisco), <u>Gefe de las tribus de esta frontera abusando del poder</u>, etc. Sonoma, Oct., 1838. Broadside.

Vallejo (Mariano G.), <u>Comandancia general de la Alta California.</u> Sonoma, Oct. 15, 1838. Broadside.

Vallejo (Mariano G.), <u>Comandancia general de la Alta California.</u> 1838. Broadside.

Vallejo (Mariano G.), <u>El señor comisionado, el supremo gobierno Don Andrés Castillero..."Tengo el honor de comunicar...".</u> Sonoma, Nov. 27, 1838. Broadside, printed both sides.

<u>Doctrina para los padres de familia, carta de una novia de moda, a su futura, contestación a la carta anterior.</u> Sonoma, 1838. Broadside. "The only specimen of poetry issued from the Spanish press of California before 1845." (Cowan)

Vallejo (Mariano G.), <u>Oficio impreso, en que quiere renunciar el mando.</u> 1838.

Alvarado (Juan Bautista), <u>Campaña de las flores.</u> 1838.

Alvarado (Juan Bautista), <u>Proclama del gefe político interino de la Alta California.</u> Sonoma, 1838. Broadside.

Arrillaga (Basilio José), <u>Recopilación de leyes.</u> 1838.

<u>Practica general de los remedios esperimentados.</u> Sonoma, 1838. 23 p. The original was printed in Cádiz, Spain.

Bustamante (Carlos María), <u>Voz de la patria, continuación.</u> 1838-39.

Alvarado (Juan Bautista), Instrucciones que deberá observar el Visitador Hartnell. 1839.

Alvarado (Juan Bautista), Reglamento provisional para administradores de misiones. 1839.

Frejes (Francisco), Historia breve de la conquista de los estados independientes de imperio mejicano. México, F. Ojeda, 1839. Reprinted in 1878. 302 p. Contains a chapter on the Californias.

Vallejo (Mariano G.), El comandante general de la Alta California. Calyfornios (sic); el gobierno francés, etc. Sonoma, June 12, 1839. Broadside.

Vallejo (Salvador), Aviso al público. Sonoma, 1839. Broadsid

Registro de licencias militares. 1839.

Guerrero (Francisco), Cartas. 1839-46.

Alvarado (Juan Bautista), Proclama del gobernador sobre destierro de extrangeros. 1840.

Alvarado (Juan Bautista), Instrucciones al prefecto Castro. 1840.

Alvarado (Juan Bautista), Suprimiendo los empleos de administradores de misiones. 1840.

Alvarado (Juan Bautista), Instrucciones que debe observar el visitador. 1840.

Reglamento para el gobierno interior de la junta departament 1840.

Vallejo (Mariano G.), Informes al ministro de guerra sobre l sublevación de Graham. 1840.

García Diego (Francisco), Carta pastoral. México, 1840. 12

Vallejo (Mariano G.), <u>Males de California y sus remedios</u>. 1841.

Bustamante (Carlos María), <u>Apuntes para la historia del gobierno del General Santa Ana.</u> 1841-43.

Bustamante (Carlos María), <u>Diario de lo especialmente ocurrido en México.</u> 1841-43.

Bustamante (Carlos María), <u>Gabinete mexicano.</u>

Alvarado (Juan Bautista), <u>Primitivo descubrimiento de oro en California.</u> 1841.

Espalda, <u>Catecismo de la doctrina cristiana.</u> Monterey, 1842. 8 p.

Micheltorena (Manuel), <u>Instrucciones</u>. 1842.

Pico (José de Jesús), <u>Mofras a San Antonio.</u> 1842.

Fondo Piadoso de Californias. 1842.

Compendio de la gramática castellana. Monterey, 1843. 67 p.

Definición de las principales operaciones de aritmética. Monterey, 1843. 26 p.

Tablas para sumar, restar y multiplicar. Monterey, 1843. 13 p.

Testo de la doctrina cristiana. Monterey, 1843. 89 p.

Micheltorena (Manuel), <u>Bando económico.</u> 1843.

Micheltorena (Manuel), <u>Decreto por el cual devuelve las misiones a los frailes.</u> 1843.

Alvarado (Juan Bautista), Reglamento de ex-misiones. 1843.

Junta consultativa y económica en Monterey. 1843.

Micheltorena (Manuel), Digest of Correspondence. 1843.

Lataillade (Cesareo) y de la Guerra (María Antonia) tienen
el honor de participar a Ud. haber celebrado matrimonio, etc. 1843 or 44. Broadside.

Micheltorena (Manuel), Oración cívica que elegido por la
junta patriótica, 27 setiembre de 1844. Monterey,
1844. 5 p.

Larkin (Thomas), Announcement of his appointment as United
States Consul to California. (in Spanish). Monterey,
April 2, 1844. Broadside.

Micheltorena (Manuel), Decreto prohibiendo la introducción
de efectos extrangeros. 1844.

Castañares (Manuel), California y sus males, exposición. 1844

Micheltorena (Manuel), Conciudadanos. 1844. Monterey.
Broadside.

Micheltorena (Manuel), Anuncia la apertura de las sesiones
de la diputación. 1844.

Micheltorena (Manuel), Decreto de la asamblea, recursos para
la guerra probable. 1844.

Micheltorena (Manuel), Reglamento de escuelas amigas. 1844.

Micheltorena (Manuel), Reglamento de milicia auxiliar.
Monterey, July 16, 1844. Broadside.

Reclamación del acto que ocupó los bienes del fondo piadoso
de Californias. México, 1845. 28 p.

ectificación de graves equivocaciones en que inciden los
    señores terceros poseedores de bienes del fondo
    piadoso de California. México, Lara, 1845.

egundo cuaderno de interesantes documentos relativos a
    los bienes del fondo piadoso de misiones. México,
    Lara, 1845. 32 p.

an Miguel (Juan Rodríguez de), Exposición a la comisión de
    hacienda de la augusta cámara de senadores a favor
    de las misiones de California, México. Mexico, Lara,
    1845, 36 p.

pia de uno de los párrafos por el exmo. señor ministro de
    relaciones exteriores. Monterey, March 12, 1845.
    Broadside.

stañares (Manuel), Colección de documentos relativos al
    departamento de Californias. México, La voz del
    pueblo, 1845. 70 p.

stillo (Felipe), Itinerario desde Sonora hasta California.
    1845.

candon (Manuel), and Rascón (José), Observaciones, fondo
    piadoso. 1845.

jar (José María), Instrucciones del gobierno al comisionado
    1845.

estra, Expedición de California. 1845.

a Miguel (Juan Rodríguez de), Documentos relativos al
    piadoso fondo de misiones de California. México,
    Luís Abadiano y Valdés, 1845. 60 p.

cripción topográfica de misiones. 1845.

ista científica y literaria de Méjico. 1845.

Reglamento de defensores de la independencia. 1845.

Castro (José), Orden del comandante general acerca de
      emigrados de los Estados Unidos. 1845.

Alvarado and Castro, Exposición contra Micheltorena. 1845.

Pico (Pío), Correspondencia con vocales recalcitrantes del
      norte. 1845.

Pico (Pío), Reglamento del gobernador para la enagenación
      y arriendo de misiones. 1845.

Restaurador (El), México. 1846.

Pronunciamiento de Varela y otros contra los americanos. 184

Pico (Pío), Decreto de abril 4, 1846.

Flores (José María), Oficios del comandante general. 1846.

Alviso (José Antonio), Campaña de Natividad. 1846.

Carrillo (José Antonio), Acción de San Pedro contra los
      americanos. 1846.

Consejo general de pueblos unidos de California. 1846.

Bandini (Juan), Proyecto de misiones. 1846.

Berreyesa and Carrillo, Quarrel at Sonoma. 1846.

Escobar (Agustín), Campaña de 1846.

Arco Iris, Vera Cruz. 1847

Castro (Manuel), <u>Carta a Don Pío Pico.</u> <u>Revolución de Flores.</u> 1847.

Castro (Manuel), <u>Informe en Sonora.</u> 1847.

Chico (Mariano), <u>Dos palabras sobre memoria del ex-gobernador Doblado.</u> 1847.

Bustamante (Carlos María), <u>El nuevo Bernal Díaz del Castillo o sea historia de la invasión de los anglo-americanos en México.</u> 1847.

Cahuenga, <u>Capitalación de 13 de enero, 1847.</u>

Flores (José María), <u>Informe al gobernador de Sonora.</u> 1847.

Flores (José María), <u>Informe de 5 de febrero, 1847, y correspondencia con las autoridades de Sonora.</u>

Rejón (Manuel C.), <u>Observaciones del diputado Salitente contra los tratados de paz.</u> 1848.

Escudero (José Agustín), <u>Memorias del diputado de Chihauhau.</u> 1848.

Guerra entre México y los Estados Unidos, apuntes. 1848

Alaman (Lucas), <u>Historia de Méjico.</u> 1849-52.

Instrucciones que los virreyes de Nueva España dejaron a sus sucesores. México, 1867. 317 p. The "In-strucciones" of Don Manuel Flores, 1789, Virrey Marquis de Branciforte, 1797, and señor Marquina, 1803, contain many references to California.

Bibliography

of

CALIFORNIA LITERATURE
PRE-GOLD   RUSH PERIOD

F R E N C.H P H A S E

French Bibliography

Wytfliet (Cornille), and Magin (Anthoine), <u>Histoire</u>
<u>universelle des Indes occidentales et orientales,</u>
<u>et de la conversion des indiens.</u> 3 parts: 108, 66,
54 pp. Douay: chez François Fabri, 1611. Map of
California opposite p. 88.

Verbiest (Père), <u>Voyages de l'Empereur de la Chine dans la</u>
<u>Tartarie, auxquels on a joint une nouvelle découverte</u>
au Méxique. 110 pp. Paris: Estienne Michallet, 1685.
"Nouvelle descente des espagnols dans l'isle de
Californie, l'an 1683," pp 79-110.

<u>Lettres édifiantes et curieuses, écrites des missions</u>
<u>étrangères par quelques missionaires de la Compagnie</u>
<u>de Jésus.</u> 288 pp. Paris: Nicolas le Clerc, 1705.
Relates partly to California. Parts republished in
Amsterdam, 1715.

Engel (Samuel), <u>Mémoires et observations géographiques et</u>
<u>critiques sur la situation des pays septentrionaux</u>
<u>de l'Asie et de l'Amérique.</u> 288 pp. Lausanne:
Antoine Chapin, 1765.

Venegas (Miguel), <u>A natural and Civil History of California.</u>
2 vols., 455, 387 pp. French edition, Paris: Durand,
1766-67.

Chappe d'Auteroche (Jean), <u>Voyage en Californie.</u> 170 pp.
Paris: C. A. Jombert, 1772.

Delaporte (M. l'Abbé), <u>Le voyageur français.</u> 468 pp.
Paris: L. Cellot, 1774. La Californie, pp 417-56.

Cortés (Hernando), <u>Correspondance de Fernand Cortés avec</u>
<u>l'Empereur Charles quint, sur la conquête de Méxique.</u>
508 pp. Paris: Cellot and Jombert, 1778-79.
California, pp 368-79.

Perouse (Jean François Galoup de la), Voyage de la Perouse
     autour du monde. 4 vols. 346, 398, 422, and 309
     pp. Atlas, 69 maps. Paris: De l'imprimerie de la
     republique, 1797.

Vancouver (George), French translations: Paris:
     De l'imprimerie de la république. 1800.

Choris (Louis), Voyage pittoresque autour du monde. Paris:
     Firmin Didot, 1822. Describes San Francisco. First
     edition, 1820.

Roquefeuil (Camille de), Journal d'un voyage autour du
     monde, pendant les années 1816-19. 2 vols., 344 and
     407 pp. Paris: Ponthieu, 1823.

Duhaut-Cilly (A), Voyage autour du monde, principalement
     à la Californie, et aux Iles Sandwich, pendant les
     années 1826-29. 2 vols., 409 and 438 pp. Paris:
     Arthus Bertrand, 1834-35.

Duflot de Mofras (Eugène), Exploration du territoire de
     l'Orégon, des Californies et de la mer Vermeille,
     exécutée pendant les années 1840-42. 2 vols., 524
     and 514 pp. Paris: Arthus Bertrand, 1844.

Montémont (Albert), De l'Orégon et de la Californie après
     les plus récentes publications sur ces contrées.
     23 pp. Paris: Société de géographie, 1846.

Bibliography

of

CALIFORNIA LITERATURE

PRE-GOLD RUSH PERIOD

DUTCH PHASE

Dutch Bibliography

Rogers (Woodes), <u>Nieuwe Reize naa de Zuidzee, 1708-11.</u>
        438 pp. Amsterdam: Johannes Oosterwyk and
        Hendrik van de Gaete, 1715.

Venegas (Miguel), <u>A Natural and Civil History of
        California.</u> 2 vols., 455 and 387 pp. Dutch edition:
        Harlem: Johann Enschede, 1761.

Bibliography

of

CALIFORNIA LITERATURE

PRE-GOLD RUSH PERIOD

G E R M A N   P H A S E

German Bibliography

Venegas (Miguel), A Natural and Civil History of California.
    2 vols., 455 and 387 pp. German edition;   Lemgo:
    Meyer, 1769-70.

Baegert (Jacob), Nachrichten von der Amerikanischen
    Halbinsel Californien. Mannheim: 1772. reprinted 1773.
    Baegert was for 18 years a Jesuit missionary in
    California. His account makes California a most
    undersirable region, utterly unfitted for human
    habitation.

Ebeling (J. P.), Le Gentils Reisen in den Indischen Meeren
    in den Jahren 1761 bis 1769, und Chappe d'Auteroche
    Reise nach Mexiko und Californien im Jahre 1769.
    Hamburg: C. E. Bohn, 1781.

Kotzebue (Otto Von), Entdeckungs-Reise in die Sud-See und
    der Berings Strasse. 3 vols., 168 pp, 176 pp, 240
    pp. Weimar, Hoffmann Gebrudern, 1821. California in
    Vol II. Contains earliest account of California
    poppy.

Kotzebue (Otto Von), Neue Reise um die Welt, in den Jahren
    1823-26. 2 vols., 191 and 177 pp. St. Petersburg:
    J. Brief, 1830. California and Russian settlement
    at Ft. Ross are described in Vol. II, pp 69-150.

<u>Bibliography</u>

of

<u>CALIFORNIA LITERATURE</u>

<u>PRE-GOLD RUSH PERIOD</u>

<u>AMERICAN and ENGLISH</u>

P H A S E

English Bibliography

Annonymous, <u>Sir Francis Drake Revived:</u>---being a summary
and true relation of four several voyages made by
the said Sir Francis Drake to the West Indies. His
encompassing the world. 4 parts, 87 pp, 108 pp,
41 pp, 60 pp. Printed at the south entrance of the
Royall Exchange, 1653.

Heylyn (Peter), <u>Cosmographie in four books containing the
chorographie and historie of the whole world, and
all the principal kingdoms, provinces, seas, and
isles thereof.</u> 4 books, 301 pp, 226 pp, 230 pp,
162 pp. London: printed for Anne Seile, (1668)-
1669. California is in book IV, pp 102-5.

Clark (Samuel), <u>The Life and Death of the Valiant and
Renowned Sir Francis Drake.</u> His voyages and discoveries in the West Indies, and about the world,
with his noble and heroic acts. 71 pp. London:
Simon Miller, 1671 "Nova Albion" (California)
described pp 29-31.

Blome (Richard), <u>Cosmography and geography in two parts.</u>
364 pp, 493 pp. London: printed by S. Roycroft for
Richard Blome (1680-) MDCLXXXII. California described as an island with cold air and ill-peopled;
pp, 451-2.

Burton (Robert), <u>The English Hero; or Sir Francis Drake
Revived.</u> Being a full account of the dangerous
voyage, admirable adventures, notable discoveries,
and magnanimous achievements of that valiant and
renowned commander, 206 pp. London: Nathaniel
Crouch, 1687. Frequently reprinted for many years.

Dampier (William), <u>A New Voyage around the World.</u> 550 pp.
Second edition, London: James Knapton, 1697. "Has
a few slight references to California, which on one
of the maps is depicted as an island."

Moll (Herman), <u>A system of Geography; or, a new and accurat
description of the earth in all its empires, kingdoms
and states.</u> 2 parts, 444 pp, 230 pp. London: Timoth
Childs, 1701. California Part I, p 177.

Cooke (Edward), <u>A Voyage to the South Sea, and Round the World, performed in the Years 1708, 1709, 1710, and 1711.</u> 2 vols., 456 and 328 pp, and maps. London: B. Lintot and R. Gosling, 1712. Cooke was captain of the Dampier expedition commanded by Woodes Rogers.

Rogers (Woodes), <u>A Cruising Voyage Round the World.</u> 428 pp. California is described pp 279-312. London: Andrew Bell, 1718. Reprinted 1739.

Picolo (Francisco Maria), <u>The Philosophical Transactions, (1700-1720).</u> Abridged and disposed under general heads, by Henry Jones. Vol. V containing pt. I and pt. II. "An account of the discoveries and settlements that Juan Maria de Salvatierra and Francisco Maria Picolo made in Lower California in 1697, contains descriptions of the natives, climate, animals, and vegetation. Pt. II, pp 191-196. Accompanying map is that of Kino, 1701." (Cowan) London: G. Strahan, 1721.

Shelvocke (George), <u>A Voyage Round the World by the Way of the Great South Sea; Performed in the years 1719, 1720, 1721; 1722.</u> 468 pp. Fullest account of California of any of the old voyages. Gold dust was discovered by the party; specimens were lost. Map shows California as an island. London: J. Senes, 1726; reprinted, London, 1757.

Betagh (William), <u>A Voyage Round the World, (1719).</u> 342 pp. California on pp 215-19. Map shows California as an island. Betagh was a member of the Shelvocke expedition. London: T. Combes, 1728.

Campbell (John), <u>A Concise History of the Spanish America.</u> 330 pp. "California and the adjacent isles," pp 83-89. London: John Stagg & Daniel Browne, 1741.

Lockman (John), <u>Travels of the Jesuits, into Various Parts of the World.</u> 2 vols., 487 and 507 pp. References to California; contains Kino map of California. London: John Noon, 1743; reprinted 1762.

Salmon (Mr.), The Modern Gazetteer: or, a Short View of the
    Several Nations of the World. "California is descri
    as an island or penninsula." The idea of California
    as an island persisted until about 1765. London:
    S. & E. Ballard, 1746.

Venegas (Miguel), A Natural and Civil History of Californi
    2 vols., 455 and 387 pp. London: James Rivington
    and James Fletcher, 1759.

Maurelle (Francisco Antonio), Journal of a Voyage in 1775,
    to Explore the Coast of America Northward of
    California. 558 pp. London: J. Nichols, 1781.

Forster (John Reinhold), History of the Voyages and
    Discoveries made in the North. 489 pp. London: 17

Vancouver (George), A Voyage of Discovery to the North
    Pacific Ocean and Round the World. 3 vols., 432, 5
    and 505 pp. London: G. G. & J. Robinson, 1798.

Perouse (Jean Francois Galoup de la), Voyage de la
    Perouse autour du monde. English translation. Lond
    J. Edwards, G. G. and J. Robinson, 1799.

Burney (James), A Chronological History of the Voyages an
    Discoveries in the South Sea or Pacific Ocean, to t
    Year 1723; including a History of the Buccaneers of
    America. An important and valuable work. London:
    Luke Hansard & Sons, 1803-17.

Rogers (Woodes), The voyage of Woodes Rogers round the
    World, with the discovery of Alexander Selkirk, the
    origin of Robinson Crusoe. 60 pp. London: Ann
    Lemoine & J. Roe, 1807.

Humbolt (Friederich Wilhelm Heinrich), Alexander, Politica
    Essay on the Kingdom of New Spain. Translated from
    the French. 4 vols. Contains references to early
    explorations in California. London: Longmans, 181

Langsdorff (Georg Heinrich Von), <u>Voyages and Travels in</u>
<u>Various parts of the World during the Years 1803-7.</u>
2 vols., 362 and 386 pp. This expedition visited
San Francisco in 1806. (Vol. II, pp 136-214. London:
Henry Colburn, 1813-14. Reprinted 1817.

Patterson (Samuel), <u>Narrative of the Adventure and Sufferings</u>
<u>of Samuel Patterson.</u> Brief mention of California.
From the Press in Palmer, May 1, 1817.

Burney (James), <u>A Chronological History of North-Eastern</u>
<u>voyages of discovery; and of the early Eastern</u>
<u>Navigators of the Russians.</u> 310 pp. London: Payne
& Foss, 1819.

Kotzebue (Otto Von), <u>Entdeckungs-Reise in die Sud-See und</u>
<u>der Berings Strasse.</u> English translation, London,
1821.

Roquefeuil (Camille de), <u>Journal d'un voyage autour du</u>
<u>monde pendant les annees 1816-19.</u> English translation,
London: Richard Phillips, 1823.

Kotzebue (Otto Von), <u>Neue Reise um die Welt, in den Jahren</u>
<u>1823-26.</u> English translations: London: Henry Colburn
& Richard Bentley, 1830.

Ranking (John), <u>Historical researches on the Conquest of</u>
<u>Peru, Mexico, Bogota, Natchez, and Tolomaco, in the</u>
<u>13th Century by the Mongols.</u> Mongols, with elephants,
land in Peru and in California. 479 pp. London:
Longmans, 1827.

Beechey (Frederick William), <u>Narrative of a Voyage to the</u>
<u>Pacific and Bering's Strait, in the Years 1825-28.</u>
2 vols., 472 and 452 pp. London: Henry Colburn &
Richard Bentley, 1831.

Pattie (James Ohio), <u>Personal Narrative.</u> 300 pp.
Cincinnati: John H. Wood, 1831; reprinted 1833,
1905, 1930.

Morrell (B), <u>A Narrative of Four Voyages to the South Sea,</u>
<u>North and South Pacific Ocean.</u> 422 pp. New York:
1832. San Diego, Monterey, etc., in 1825.

Coulter (Dr. Thomas), <u>Notes on Upper California.</u> In
journal proceedings of the Royal Geographic Society.
pp 59-70. London: 1835.

Ruschenberger (William S. W.), <u>Narrative of a Voyage round</u>
<u>the World, during the Years 1835-1837.</u> 2 vols., 450
and 472 pp. Observations on California. Vol. II, pp
402-25. London: Richard Bentley, 1838.

Forbes (Alexander), <u>California: A history of Upper and</u>
<u>Lower California from their first discovery to the</u>
<u>present time.</u> 352 pp. The first English book re-
lating exclusively to California. London: Smith,
Elder, & Co., 1839.

Leonard (Zenas), Trapper and Trader. <u>Narrative of the</u>
<u>adventures of Zenas Leonard.</u> 87 pp. The party
spent most of the winter of 1833-34 in California,
principally at Monterey. Clearfield, Pa.: D. W.
D. W. Moore, 1839. Reprinted, Cleveland, Ohio,
Burrows Bros., 1904.

Annonymous, "<u>Thirty-six Years of Sea-faring Life,</u>" by an
<u>Old Quartermaster.</u> 336 pp. The author visited
San Francisco in 1826; later touched at Monterey.
Portsea: W. Woodward, 1839.

Bennett (Frederick Debell), <u>Narrative of a Whaling Voyage</u>
<u>round the Globe, from the year 1833 to 1836.</u> 2 vols.
402 and 395 pp. Contains a sketch of California.
London: Richard Bentley, 1840.

Dana (Richard Henry, Jr.), <u>Two Years before the Mast.</u>
483 pp. Edition of 1869 contains the narrative of
second visit to California made in 1859. First
printed New York: Harpers, 1840.

Greenhow (Robert), <u>Memoir, Historical and Political, on</u>
<u>the Northwest Coast of North America, and the</u>
<u>Adjacent Territories.</u> 228 pp. Washington: Blair &
Rives, 1840.

Cleveland (Richard J.), <u>A narrative of voyages and</u>
<u>commercial enterprises.</u> 2 vols., 249 and 244 pp.
Cleveland arrived in San Diego, March, 17, 1803.

Belcher (Edward), <u>Narrative of a voyage round the World,</u>
<u>1836-42.</u> 2 vols., 387 and 474 pp. London: Henry
Colburn, 1843.

Jones (Thomas Ap Catesby), <u>Taking of Monterey.</u> 117 pp.
Washington: Government Printing Office, 1843.

Marryat (Frederick), <u>Narrative of the Travels and Adventures</u>
<u>of Monsieur Violet in California, Sonora, and Western</u>
<u>Texas.</u> 3 vols. 312, 318 and 299 pp. London: Longman,
Brown, Green; Longmans, 1843. New York: Harpers,
1843.

Farnhan (Thomas Jefferson), <u>Travels in the Californias, and</u>
<u>Scenes in the Pacific Ocean.</u> 416 pp. "Several
editions under various titles followed." Cowan.
New York: Saxton & Miles, 1844.

Greenhow (Robert), <u>The History of Oregon and California.</u>
492 pp. Boston: Little & Brown, 1845.

Wilkes (Charles), <u>Narrative of the United States Exploring</u>
<u>Expedition during the years 1838-42.</u> 6 vols. In
1840-41 the expedition visited Oregon and California.
Philadelphia: Lee & Blanchard, 1845.

Fremont (John Charles), <u>Report of the exploring expedition</u>
<u>to the Rocky Mountains in the year 1842; and to</u>
<u>Oregon and North California in the years 1843-44.</u>
583 pp. Printed by order of the House of
Representatives. Washington: Blair & Rivers, 1845.
Many prints issued.

Greenhow (Robert), <u>The Geography of Oregon and California.</u>
42 pp. New York: Mark H. Newman, 1845.

Hastings (Lansford W.), <u>The Emigrant's Guide to Oregon and</u>
California. 152 pp. Cincinnati: George Conclin, 1842.

Gilliam (Albert M.), (U. S. Consul to California Republic)
Travels over the Table Lands and Cordilleras of
Mexico, during the years 1843 and 1844; including
a description of California. 455 pp. Philadelphia:
John W. Moore, 1846.

Johnson (Overton), and Winter, (William H.) Route across the
Rocky Mountains, with a description of Oregon and
California. 152 pp. Lafayette, Ind.: John B. Seman,
1846.

Mitchell (S. Augustus), Accompaniment to Mitchell's new Map
of Texas, Oregon, and California. 46 pp. Philadelphia:
S. A. Mitchell, 1846.

Robinson (Alfred), Life in California. 226 pp. New York:
Wiley & Putnam, 1846.

Sage (Rufus B.), Scenes in the Rocky Mountains, and in
Oregon, California, New Mexico, Texas, and the
Grand Prairies. 303 pp. Philadelphia: Carey &
Harte, 1846. Several times reprinted.

Shively (J. M.), Route and distances to Oregon and
California. 15 pp. Washington, D.C.: William
Greer, 1846.

Annonymous, "Alta California," by A Captain of Volunteers.
64 pp. Philadelphia: Packer & Co., 1847.

Coulter (John, M.D.), Adventures on the Western Coast of
South America, and the Interior of California. 2 vols.,
288 and 278 pp. London: Longman, 1847.

Coyner (David H.), The Lost Trappers. 255 pp. Cincinnati:
J. A. & U. P. James, 1847.

Heustis (Daniel D.), Narrative of the Adventures and
Sufferings of Captain D.D. Heustis and His
Companions. Includes travels in California. 168 pp.
Boston: Redding & Co., 1847.

Bryant (Edwin), <u>What I Saw in California.</u> A journal of
    travel. 455 pp. New York: Appleton, 1848.

Foster (G. G.), <u>The Gold Regions of California.</u> 80 pp.
    New York: Dewitt & Davenport, 1848.

Sherwood (J. Ely), <u>California: Her Wealth and Resources.</u>
    40 pp. New York: George F. Nesbitt, 1848.

Torrey (William), <u>Torrey's Narrative.</u> 300 pp. The author
    visited California in 1837. pp 180 to 183. Boston:
    A. J. Wright, 1848.

Brooks (J. Tyrwhitt), <u>Four Months Among the Gold-Finders in
    California.</u> A diary. 94 pp. New York: Appleton,
    1849.